T0374039

My Heart Will Go On

You must have known how shocked I would be when I received your letter...my heart stopped...and for a moment I was frozen...I found myself standing on a cobble-stoned walkway... feeling...surreal... and...astounded... (Sept 14th)

AuthorHouse™
1663 Liberty Drive
Bloomington, IN 47403
www.authorhouse.com
Phone: 1-800-839-8640

Images taken from: VintageHolidayCrafts.com
Cover Image: Angel Blue Sad Mourning courtesy of Kathy Fornal @ Fine Art America
Inside Cover Image: Luthien Thye "My Heart Will Go On" Mixed Media Journal Malaysia

Published by AuthorHouse 12/22/2014

ISBN: 978-1-4969-4887-8 (sc)
978-1-4969-5041-3 (e)

Any people depicted in stock imagery provided by Thinkstock are models, and such images are being used for illustrative purposes only. Certain stock imagery © Thinkstock.

This book is printed on acid-free paper.

authorHOUSE®

Secret, Sacred, Love Letters

A TREASURE TROVE OF D E S I R E

*With facsimiles of real letters and quotations
from the author's correspondence spanning
over four decades*

*Do you mind if I write you a
love letter? I could write my
own epistle of you... (smile)...
Just on my mind...I was sitting
here at 9:06 p.m. on a Monday
night thinking of you... rainy
night in Seattle... (Dec 28th)*

Hollye Lexington

Contents

Love is the criterion for stepping up in my space and into my life...I've had my heart broken so badly, THAT I never want to experience. again...when I received that letter from you...I literally got up from my desk, walked outside don't know how because I remember my thighs growing ever so numb...thought I was dreaming...went back to the letter only to find those words were as real as you are...(Sept 10th)

I asked, no begged God for you...(April 18th)

Prologue

Reaching out to you...?
Show me how...I want to...
I would be remised if I didn't tell
You...I'm not afraid of you, that is, I
don't think I am...but I am afraid of
how you make me feel...the way you look
at me mesmerizing...do you have any
idea how drawn I am to you? And the
truth is...well... (Sept 14th)

You are so kind...
there is gentleness
about you that I have
always been drawn to...
please don't ever change.
know you have loved me...
babe the feelings were always
mutual...and reaching out to you
scares me because you just
might reach back... (Sept 14th)

I WILL REACH CAREFULLY...IF I DO...AND GENTLY.
(SEPT14)

Alfred Lord Tennyson
From his poem In Memoriam: 27, 1850:
I hold it true, whate'er befall;
I feel it, when I sorrow most;
'Tis better to have loved and lost
Than never to have loved at all.

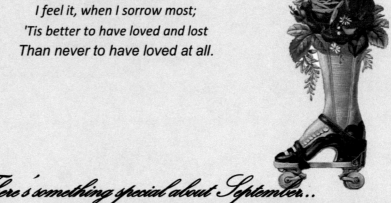

There's something special about September...

Seasons Linens

Artist: Alfonse Marie Mucha
Dedicatorial Poem by Author & Poemist Antwan Hannah

In winter when the bears have returned to the caves and the birds have flown to warmer climates, I will escape to the fireplace and cuddle next to you.

Wrapped in linen; sips of wine, I find refuge in the one who keeps the fire burning bright. When the smell of pine from the Christmas tree fills the room, we will know the meaning of love.

Roars come at midnight and with hearing strained, your heart is heard only as we countdown to something new. As we dance the night away into newness, we find love in the comfort of each other's arms. The meeting of our lips is the mood felt throughout that trigger a series of imitations that will last till spring.

When spring comes, there is nothing more I like than to picnic with you beneath the wings of a sour cherry tree. When she rattles her leaves and covers us with white snow, I see the beauty she bestows upon your face.

As we lay with wine, crackers and fruits of spring, we are serenaded by the sounds of lovebirds resting high upon a branch. They love like we and we like them; nothing more could bring delight as the suns light sparkling from your eyes. We'll love this way into summer

When summer arrives, I imagine waking in morning bliss in a lavish room that is caressed by the scenes of the sea. As we walk the shores with sand between our toes, we skip rocks in a weird lovers exchange and I give chase after you back to the waves that chase me. In the arms of sand we love like this into fall

When fall brought the dancing leaves of beautiful trees that will soon fade to sleep, we dance along with them in rhythm becoming one with the subtle wind that tickle our nose. In the air the fragrance of your perfume lingers as the trees bow in pleasure knowing their leaves will not fall in gloom. When night falls asleep till winter; the chimney lit with the smell of maple wood burning. Our wine glasses we be filled as we lay comforted in each other's arms happily under the imaginative cloak of season linen.

The Betrayal

The Betrayal...

How could you disclose our private love letters? I wish I'd never met you! You promised to take care of my heart! What a horrible crime that has been committed and celebrated! At the expense of what? Certainly to have our love letters exposed for this herd you call friends to voraciously mock for their own pleasure, hurts like hell! Such private and intimate thoughts that should have gone with you to your grave! But I'll give you a standing ovation my love! Props to you and the demon you rode in on! After all this time, after all these years! And why should I be so freaking surprised? This was all done so insidiously! I hate you now! Our precious love letters...violated! What kind of creature are you? And they laughed! In my face! And had the audacity to repeat my intimate letters! Verbatim! What a Travesty! How can you take something so beautiful...? If I were God your hell would be redefined!!! How could you mock a love you claim you've always wanted, and for years? They accused me of worshipping you...and I did worship the man in you, only because you worshipped me first!!! If they only knew! I hate what you have done now! Our precious love letters...a sacred thing...I didn't know my heart was being led to the slaughter...and all you can say is "I'm sorry." Why my luv? Why? Even in all this...I found the strength to forgive you! But I will never, ever allow you into my heart...or life....again! Ever! (Dec 30th)

Private love letters disclosed...
Revealed this time...with CLASS...

My Manasseh Season

There are gifts from God...

then there's you...

I'm a blessed man... (Jul 16ᵗʰ)

Love hearing you tell me you love me...every conversation, every time you are near...I feel like I'm coming into my own Manasseh season as Joseph did...Manasseh...Made to Forget... Oh my dear...it is because of you I have literally forgotten the pain and heartbreak of yesterday...the sting of it has been removed from my heart...I know that because my heart feels free and it is about to burst! In a good way...God knows how to make it up to you for all the pain you've suffered in the past...I believe as Joseph did...that God has established this thing...and everything that happened up to this point...even when I didn't understand...when my why's were not answered...I never thought in my wildest dream that I could have favor with you...my knees are trembling even now...only God could do this thing...only God...could take the most powerful force in the world and trust me with it...even when I didn't trust myself...but He trusted me and 'made me forget'...I have experienced you and I've never met anyone like you...I do know this that I will love you for the rest of my life, you are here and I am so grateful...utterly grateful....(Oct 29ᵗʰ)

"To every thing there is a season, and a time to every purpose under the heaven..." Ecclesiastes 3:1a

Enamored

Then...I have always loved you...please...
whatever you need...anything...just reach.
(Sept.14th)

God I love this man! (Sept 14th)

The last time I saw you and we were at my place. I was so glad you were there....while standing at my front door as I helped you put your jacket on I realized that I didn't want you to leave...and when you left there was this emptiness...I knew then as I know now...that I'd fallen in love with you... (Jun 25th)

I'm not fighting myself anymore... (Aug 29th)

Want to cherish you...until forever... (May 19th)

**My love is hopeless, helpless and homeless without you...
(Sept 19th)**

YOU ARE DEARER TO ME THAN ANYONE I HAVE EVER KNOWN... (FEB 3RD)

There is a sweetness to every encounter
with you... (June 4th)

I have found the one whom my soul loves...
(Songs of Solomon 3:4v)

You must have told me you loved me a million times…and a million times
I have screamed… (Dec 3rd)

Yes, I desire to spend time with you…I'm not placid for God's sake…I fell in love with being in your arms…I loved listening to you sleep and you didn't snore (smile…well not this time)…I love being watched by you…I wish I could lay in your lap and listen to you whisper the things that are on the table of your heart…I love touching you… and I crave to know what you smell like…you should know me by now…me and my overactive imagination…tasting you is what I desire the most…love kissing your mouth! I believe making love to you would definitely satisfy my frustrations but that would simply send me further into this abyss…I'm sorry if you feel I'm being too forward…as I stated, you should know me by now… (Nov 10th)

When I die men are going to run and spit on my grave! I'm so damned good to you! Nobody will ever love you like I do! You are spoiled! Ruined! All mines! Even after I'm dead and gone! (Aug 14th)

Babe, Thank you for the beautiful flowers… (April 5th)

You can never leave me… (April 5th)

Smitten...

I could look at you forever ... (Sept

You are extra-ordinarily beautiful to me, to me.... (July 5th)

Just thinking how wonderful you were today...and looked it too...
(May 15th)

Thank you for the other night...you were wonderful...my heart races with every aftershock...and I keep waiting for them to subside...but...they haven't, honestly I don't want them to...I've never felt more like a woman in my life...hope I made you happy even in the midst of mixed emotions...I'm not sad...how could I be? I Love being with you... (March 19th)

I LOOK AT YOU SOMETIMES AND I SAY TO MYSELF, HE DOESN'T KNOW... THAT I LOVE HIM SO MUCH...THAT I CARE... (JAN 20TH)

When I'm with you or on the phone with you, I'm often so nervous that I can't think…my brain goes blank…as much as I talk…somehow something manages to come out of my mouth…my heart speaking about the way I feel about you…whether I miss you, love you, or want to see you…and I am not ashamed… (Sept 18th)

"How beautiful you, my love! How beautiful you are! Your eyes are like doves."
Songs of Solomon 1:15v

Walking through my house calling your name…and you are not even here…
(Sept 27th)

You are one of the most beautiful women in the world… to me…TO ME… (Aug 16th)

Wear that black velvet dress again please…my, my, my… I dreamed about you last night in that black velvet dress…I am sweet as hell on you and you know it. (Jun 27th)

You don't know how many times I have watched you; how many times I have possessed you…in my mind; I have fantasied about you too many times to number. How many times I have pondered…how I have ruminated over you in the night? I said to myself, she does not have a clue what she is to me…in my mind. You are everything! Now I have the privilege of telling you…to your face… Oh Happy Day! (Jul 29th)

AFTeRsHoCkS!

I was never afraid of you...but I was always afraid of how you made me feel...there is a place you can reach...as a blind man...unaware if the next step is solid ground or if the next step is off a cliff...so what do I do? Not take the next step? Well, I'm not afraid anymore...because the times we've spent together, the void in my life was filled, the emptiness...filled...you made me feel like I belong and that it's okay to be me... nobody else would understand. I've always wanted to belong...I'm fulfilled when you're with me but when you're not around nothing's the same ...

I never said I was finished with you...I just want someone in my life that's here, someone that's consistent...someone that I love...in the midst of busy living, someone I can take care of...laugh with in the wee hours of the morning...wash your back for you...play strip poker with...trade lap dances...kiss until our lips go numb again...play hide-n-go-uh-huh...talk politics with...shoot hoops with...cook for...sing to...let you kiss my feet(you do it so well)...rub your head until you fall asleep in my lap...make love until my tears make you stop...whisper in your ear all the things I've been waiting to tell you... I only love you... if you had nothing, so what your name is not in lights, if nobody's ever heard of you...if you are you... the same man...I would love you for the rest of my life and then forever after that...you were the man in my dreams with no face...but I asked God for you...someone tangible in the earth realm...it's the man in you that I've waited my whole life for...my love for you will never be hidden, lost or finished ...it's the kind of love that even death will have no dominion over...it's not that deep...I'm just saying...you are my "aftershock"...
Love you until time stands still... (Feb 4th)

THE WAY YOU MAKE ME FEEL IS OFF THE RICHTER SCALE! MY

DESIRES... AND THERE ARE MANY...

ARE FOR YOU AND YOU ALONE!

(JUL 5TH)

Ravishing

My biggest fear is...that I will love you too much!

My question has always been... how do I continue to restrain myself? I cannot ignore you... (Jan 9th)

Telling me not to love is like trying to tell the sun not to shine... (Feb 6th)

How do I not show how crazy I am about you? A part of me wants to go mad for you...desire pent up...is like a bursting dam... (May 25th)

I DECLARE

THAT YOU

ARE THE

GREAT

LOVE

OF MY

LIFE...

(SEPT 30TH)

You kiss every inch of my face as if it were something to be consumed...I love it...don't you dare stop...giving me all this love becomes you...you wear love well...every second with you is memorable...nothing is wasted, no time, no love, no wine...you are such a joy sweetheart...(May 18th)

You are my beloved...I have been yearning to meet you for 4,748 days...since the first day I saw you, I can predict your every gesture; if you will turn left or right; I know the exact moment you squint your eyes; love the way you sway your round hips...it seems that I am the only man In all the world who is bothered by your flowy blonde curls, so beautiful, seductive; help me not go mad...if I were ever to become disenchanted by your sweetness...I would decree myself an unfinished man...I must have you...(Jun 24th)

I just want you around... (Jul 7th)

Many sleepless nights I've pensively pondered in my hearts mind about you...I knew I was falling in love with you because I want to make love to you incessantly, insatiably, and incoherently...in the sweetest way...
(Oct 4ᵗʰ)

I need you to sweetly ravish me...please...

I've been waiting, and praying...

An awful long time...

I pray, should that day ever come...

That I don't overwhelm you... your presence alone stirs me...you excite me...

(Jun 8ᵗʰ)

I go crazy whenever I see you, you know that…you make me want to feel all of you…I love being on my knees before you…the pleasure is so rich…yes I love God…I love you too…I'm ravished!

(Mar 11ᵗʰ)

It's almost 4am...can't sleep...I was anxious to see you, why didn't you call to say were not coming? You are dear to my heart, know that I would rather die a thousand deaths than to hurt you, regardless to what my friends and the enemy has said...I care about you...and I want you in my life....All I have to offer is my love...for the rest of your life, love you and take care of you like the king that you are... (Mar 7ᵗʰ)

Let him kiss me with the kisses of his mouth for your love is more delightful than wine. (Songs of Solomon 1:2v)

MESMERIZED

I can't keep my eyes off you…in public I'm a mess…(Feb 5th)

You're an overwhelming woman! (Sept 19th)

I'm crazy about you woman…(Dec 23rd)

My love doesn't come cheap…and that you're worth it. (Sept 19th)

YOU ARE A RARITY MY SUGAR…(May 19th)

Babe,

…love the way your breath smells….and the way you look at me…oh my… Mesmerizing…do you have any idea how drawn I am to you? And the truth is…well…your arms, your arms… (Jul 23rd)

I want you to know what last Saturday meant to me…if I can find the words…it was exactly what I asked God for…how I have fantasized about us…you always make me feel like a woman… (Sept 27th)

Love touching you…looking into your face…kissing you…I didn't want to leave…every moment with you is mind blowing…You were like a beautiful surprise…sighing…thank you for being so sweet to me on my mom's birthday…may she rest in peace…love the way you comfort me… (Oct 12th)

You love me so openly and so conspicuously…I'm always in blush mode and with butterflies in my belly… (Sept 23rd)

I don't know what's going to happen...you've been on my heart and mind so strongly...can I love you this much? Yes I can and yes I do... Isn't it amazing...the one thing I asked God for...it shows up...and I begin to struggle with it...that shouldn't be...I can't run from it...because I can't run from myself...but it's the unknown that scares me so...I never knew you could mean so much to me...I didn't plan it...it just happened...and I'm glad it did...and I want to see you always... (Feb 2nd)

Love the first time you kissed me sitting on the love stool...

It was the initial "I have always loved you That got me... and every

"I love you"

after that...(Jun 6th)

Remember those days at the
Beach my dear? I remember how
I curled next to you as we drank wine
and snacked on cheese. You held me
so tight as the waves crashed over and
over...the beach goers were so friendly...
you must have kissed me a thousand times...(Nov 13th)

How'd you get so fine? (Mar 8th)

MY GOD IN
HEAVEN... I
AM TOTALLY
MESMERIZED
BY YOU...
DYING TO
POSSESS
YOU...

I could look into your eyes forever...I search for that moment, when your eyes meet mines...something volcanic arises in me...(Sept 10th)

(FEB 24TH)

Just wanna hold you girl right now at 4 o'clock in the morning... and never let you go... (Mar 6th)

I S A T I A B L E

I N S A T I A B L E

YOUR ARE:

EATABLE!

LOVABLE!

LIKEABLE!

DESIRABLE

EXCITABLE!

INIMITABLE
IRRESISTBLE
PLEASURABLE!

IRREPLACABLE!

Can't sleep! If I do fall asleep at night, I am awakened by you…2a.m.…..3a.m. thoughts of you…see your beautiful face…it's this incessant longing for you that drives me absolutely crazy… (Dec 1ˢᵗ)

The perfume of your sweetness tells me that your mother must have feasted on pineapples and Chrysanthemums…

I'll tell you something that's surely of a rarity…for me that is, is the fact that…I miss you…I…miss you…I do…not the norm for me…How did I get here? Don't know…really don't care…but to be satisfied with seeing you again means the world to me… (Sept 26ᵗ)

You appease me in a way no other human being has…ever! I can't get enough…God what have I done to be loved in this way? Thank you…God…
(Apr 24ᵗʰ)

Can't sleep…what time are you coming home? (Sept 19ᵗʰ)

"His mouth is most sweet, and he is altogether desirable." (Songs of Solomon 5:16)

I want to look at you forever…and always want you here with me…how long have I dreamt of making love with you? You please me and I love you for that…I can still feel you in my arms, love holding you so tightly and whispering in your ears…how I praised God in those moments when you are with me…everything is alright…go right ahead and scream…want to love you and never stop….can I have you in my life forever? Adore you, I do…I expected you to be sweet as honey to me…how is it that I never quite believe that you are you….smothering me with sweet kisses…I cherish you…love sharing time with you, it makes it all worth it….I thank God for having made you, thanking Him that I love you with all my heart and soul, above all thanking Him because he has permitted you to love me…know that you are unparalleled to none…with a beautiful mind…I love you so much more today than I did a week ago…(Aug 8th)

If you tell me no…then it's no….period..And its okay…that's from a real man… (Sept 22nd)

I'm afraid I'll awaken and find all this a dream…then let me sleep…what a treasure to possess…I've been searching for the heart of my heart…have I found it? You set me in a place that no other woman can touch me…I've been waiting for you…shall I find grace and favor in your sight…?…every inch of me…is stimulated when you walk into a room and know this…that I love loving you …I love you overwhelmingly, insatiably, passionately and flirtatiously…you're still my baby.. Adore you… (Dec 28th

Show me how to love you and not miss you…teach me to long for you every day and night but not need to hold you…convince me that I can love you insanely and not touch you for weeks at a time…show me how to make love to you and get up the same way I laid down…teach me how to love you and let go until the next time I see you…I want you in my life…but I don't know how to love you and not show it…how do I love you and not fall in love with you even more every time I see you? Forgive me please…it's because all of my life I've been waiting for you…you…didn't know what type of package you would come wrapped in…all my life I've wanted this type of love…please don't get tired of me pulling on your heart…I want to come in…I need you…you are the part of me that I never want to let go of… I just want to know and feel that you love me… future desires are so strong…I love you to the point of passion that unhinges my soul…, that's a place I want to be…to love you just like that…it's not crazy to me, it's where I need to be…you are dearer to me than any person I've ever known…in truth you are extraordinarily beautiful…I feel like you are here because I dreamt you up…consecrated only to you…let me love you …I'm wandering…please don't let me wander…can we make love again? All I want to think about is you and no one else… (Feb 3d)

Yes, baby girl, this is real… (Sept 25th)

Tell me what to do...nights are as days and days are as nights...I can't sleep girl...
If I wake up another morning wanting you the way I have been these past few
days I think I might go insane...

I want you...

I can't distinguish if its lust or if I love you so, like that...
I'm not trying to tempt you...perhaps you were my last thoughts when I finally
drifted off to sleep...perhaps this escalation of desire was increased by my need
to see you...my concern is when I'm awakened by my own moaning because I need
you so...I could feel your presence to strongly...

I want you...

Tell me what to do...I'm not asking you for a remedy...
No matter how busy I get my need for you is still there...can't get enough
of you, your laugh, your smile, you...crazy about you...

(Jul 24th)

I'M

INSATIABLE
INSATIABLE

Addicted!

I need a habit...I long to be addicted to something wonderful tangible...I can be real spoiled sometimes I know...but there's nobody sweeter, I promise....insipid I'll never be...incessant I'll admit...these lonely nights and mornings are calling me...I'm drawn to you by reason of your qualitative obsession with...well...I'm addicted to you...you are my...perfect habit... (Aug 14th)

BABYYYYYYYY! WHERE ARE YOU? COME OVER HERE NOW! I NEED YOU! I'LL SEND A CAB; TRAIN...JUST GET OVER HERE! (Oct 7th)

I CRAVE FOR YOU...(SEPT 30TH)

Babe...

this

City

IS a

morgue

without

you...

(Nov 16th)

WHEN·SHALL·WE
THREE·MEET·AGAIN?

Oh God I miss you! Help me please...I miss you so much... I've been assessing the cost and the value of the love I have for you...there is a difference you know? How can I love you so much with all these limits? How can I express myself freely with all these chains? Is love bound? Can love be bound? And then how can I ever love you in its fullest when you're so far away? I love this season of my life...why? Because you're in it...I just want to hold you the way you've always held me...you're the only one I know that allows me to be me...and you don't freak out...if I want to get on my knees before you...and I have...you allow it...if I want to kiss every inch of your face...and I have...you let me...when I say I'm lonely for you, know it...I go into a whole other dimension when I'm with you or just thinking of you...everything in me longs for you...my ears long to hear your voice...my hands long to touch you...my eyes long to see you...my mouth needs to kiss yours...my arms long to hold you...my body sweetly, intensely desires yours...and I just want to touch you...many times this whole experience seems so surreal to me...no doubt it's because I've been the needing you all my life. And to have a blessing in my arms of this magnitude...literally blows my mind...I want to see you every day...I want you in my life forever...I need you in my life...do you understand? I'm addicted to you I know! What must I do? How? I need you to be free ...to allow your heart to love me...you reached for me and I reached back...you awakened the seducer in me again and again...most of my pain came when I tried not to love you...my body aches for your hands, for your mouth...I love you...what do I do when I am desperately climbing the walls at 3 o'clock in the morning? No you are not God but some of my prayers YOU can answer...What do I do when these feelings won't subside...and I'm crazier about you today than I was yesterday? You're always on my mind...even when I try not to think of you...even when I purposely overload my daily agenda...I can't stop thinking about you...and I've told you once and I'll tell you twice...babe...this City IS a morgue without you...please come home soon...wanna hold you so bad...you are my daily fix! You are my addiction....I now understand the loving someone throughout infinity... to spend the rest of your life with...the cost of my love? I would give up everything...for you... (Nov 16th)

These four days seem like four years since I left you in Cali...my soul misses you...I know, I know...I must endure just a few more days...thank God for memories...if I should ever lose my memories of you...oh God forbid...I shall hurry home...I have to go... The cabin door is closed...(Jan 25th)

So the man I dreamed about my whole life does exist! I'm hoping ☺ *...Just the mere hope...an inkling...a hint of my dream being a reality enlivens me...I love that you are here...I'm am ecstatic at the thought that perhaps, you just might be him...I can't wait to see you again...and I want you...always...It's the kind of dream...that makes me want to live at your feet...and die in your arms...So it's no spell...it's called...love...it's called...forever...My heart loves you...***I'm under no spell...but being in love...is...a spell... (Dec 3rd)***

I've reached back so hard for you until I feel it in the core of my soul…in my inner bowels…I've never been here before but I can taste a sweetness…I'd better behave before you start fussing at me again…gonna try to get some sleep…schedule calls for an early rise…remember me… (Nov 30th)

RESCUE ME!
NOT HIGH OFF OF
A FANTASY...YOU
ARE HERE AND
YOU ARE
REAL...YOU LOVE
TOO HARD....
I THINK I NEED
AN
INTERVENTION...
(JUN 8TH)

HANGOVERS ARE NOT SUPPOSED
TO LAST THIS LONG...YOU ARE IN
MY SPIRIT... (JAN 19TH)

Why did you leave without waking me? I turned over and you were gone...I rolled over to the spot where you laid...I could still feel you...smell you...I am sincerely intoxicated...everything in me announces the obvious fact that you are no longer in my space...but I close my eyes and see you...I feel your overwhelming kiss on my tender lips.... and the world is but a blur to me... you are my aching addiction...I can't wait to have you right here with me again...(Aug 6th)

It is not true that love will cause you to change? Love cannot be hidden...in the sense that you don't have to open your mouth...it speaks volumes...they say we have a lot of passion between us...all I am sure of is the way that my heart melts when you call my name...it's hard to remember anything after that! (Jun 25)

Awakened this morning at 5:19a.m. with you bursting out from my thoughts...I don't mind, long as my thoughts of you remain pleasant...and they have...so I won't abandon them...however I feel an addiction coming on...

I'm always seeking my first high with you...most people are addicted to a thing because they haven't found anything better...perhaps I have found the 'better thing'. Still reeling...

My first high with you...totally was syncope...every time you touched me... I whisper my addiction to you...

I believe it was J.Z. Knight that said, "You can't cure an addict, just give them everything they want until they want no more." Is there such a thing with you as not wanting no more?

Can I overdose on this guy?

Intoxicated by your smell...(Oct 2ˢᵗ)

I am not consumed...not totally, yet...can I be addicted and not be totally consumed by you?
I've become addicted to my own thoughts of you...how do you diagnose my addiction?

Pardon me for being such a girl right now okay...but the next time you decide to wake me @ 5 a.m. in the morning talking that talk and promising to drive me crazy...please make sure you're near...I was a mess...need you like that...Always...

(Jan 5ᵗʰ)

Worshipping

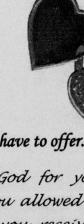

Love is all I have to offer. (Apr 14ᵗʰ)

I thank God for you...you are my dream...you allowed me to kiss your feet and you received me gently...I want to kiss them all over...I'm happy you are in my life...now that you're here I never want you to leave...please remember me...keep me close...I don't want to lose you...ever...(Oct 29ᵗʰ)

I love looking at those feet...kissing those feet...love those feet...smile (Jul 17ᵗʰ)

"He brought me to the banqueting house, and his banner over me was love."

Songs of Solomon 2:4v (Dec 23ʳᵈ)

Have our souls met? (Apr 2ⁿᵈ)

I trust you with my heart... (Feb 2nd)

I Simply Adore You... (Nov 23ʳᵈ)

How surprising that I am speechless whenever I hear your voice on the other end of the phone? How my mind experiences a syncope episode when you hold me...you always hold me so tight, as if you are trying to merge our bodies into one...no man has ever held me like that...don't stop... (Feb 27ᵗʰ)

I VENERATE YOU... (OCT 13ᵀᴴ)

You are the BEST THING that has happened to me in years my dear... (Sept 23ʳᵈ)

Promise to return the favor one day...I remember you and I down in your din dancing to the Commodores "Easy"...We had a blast.... glad dancing wasn't a sin to you (smile)...I remembering clapping for you as you did your solo dance for me...sooo much fun... I remember looking up to you with tears in my eyes, oh how you make me laugh, until my face hurts...

I was so happy to be there with you because it was right and I knew it...my favorite spot in your house is the fireplace and I Remember how intimate and cozy it was sitting there with you listening to you whisper wonderful things to me...

I remember every smile you've given me...I remember how affectionate you were with me, touching my hair and how tight you held me until I couldn't breathe....I remember how you kept telling me how beautiful I was, I never felt more beautiful than every time I was with you...and I was in the place that I've dreamed of all my life...with you. I remember sitting on your couch and you telling me so many secret things of your love for me over the years....from that day I never wanted to leave you...I remember following you from your home as you led me back to the main road, you rolled down your window and told me you loved me for the first time and I told you I loved you too...for the first time...awesome first date...Thank you for the Antinori Solaia wine...delightful! (Jan 2ˢᵗ)

I'm a man...I loved you before I ever met you...

God has heard my prayers... (Feb 8ᵗʰ)

"Just allow love to lead us...naturally"... (Nov 9ᵗʰ)

My beloved is to me a sachet of myrrh that lies between my breasts." (Songs of Solomon 1:13v)

And every day I want to see you...yes I'm crazy...By the way I meant to ask you if you would marry me... no I haven't been drinking although that sounds very tempting at the moment...it's better to marry than to burn...and I've become an inextinguishable wild fire...you're driving me crazy...(Sept 30ᵗʰ)

Is not love the chalice of the heart?

Hey honey... It's late... It's 3 o'clock in the morning... I dreamt it was raining outside...It was only a dream...Then I was awakened with thoughts of you...All pleasurous of course Smile... my definition: pleasurous = incessant sensual gratification... Your arms are my heaven...You keep asking me if I love you...Can I love you anymore? Thoughts of you in the night speak volumes to me....how frightening at times to think...well... There is no bottom to my love for you...yet...Are you the face to my prayers? If I told you of my dreams would you laugh at me? Can I allow you to experience me even on a deeper level and not be ashamed? Is there a confidante in you for me? (Sept 18th)

Loving you is comparable to diving into a pool of rosewater...drown me in it...can anything else be so delicious to me? I think not! You are so damned refreshing! I like it! I love it! I will never tire of it! You are my heaven! Redoubled! (Dec 23rd)

Nothing and nobody else exists when you are near...your favor means everything to me...everything... (Oct 5th)

Thank you for praying for me... (June 21st)

YOUR WORDS, ARE JOLTING...I KNOW YOU ARE NOT A FEROCIOUS WOLF!
YOU ARE SWEET AS A HONEYCOMB TO ME... (NOV 29TH)

How I long to be at your mercy in the sweetest way and know that you will take care of me...You always do...I cannot get that image out of my heart nor head of you kneeling before me in the apartment...I wanted to scream...I just want to hold you...Forever...I'm intoxicated with you...I can't help but want more ...I want you...I'm sorry...Not trying to tempt you...If only all acts of love were pure...Fulfill me...Please...Must I beg? I will...I can't escape the conviction...I can't escape the guilt...Neither can I escape this devastatingly, insatiable, passionate, yet tormentous need for you which screams at me from beneath my facades...Not seeing you is like hell! Wanting you to touch me and kiss me everywhere...I love the way you look at me when we are face to face...I love smelling your breath on my face...And your arms are my heaven...That's the one place I never ever want to leave...You can't love me like that and forget about me ...I reach for you because I have no other choice...Fulfill me...Please...Am I asking too much? I'll keep asking ...What would I not do for your love? And yes I can love you more...So much more...And I want to...And yes...I still love you...you are heaven to me... (Dec 11th)

Conflict

"Love Among the Ruins"

...hurting right now...I'm sorry my love...

we tried...real love would have survived...(Feb 28ᵗʰ)

You and all your drama! Such a farce! I don't live like this!
(Nov 29th)

Would I keep straining for you? Reaching for someone that was not good for me? And I know! I've known it all along! But you're wonderful! Wonderful...but you live in a chained heart...
(October 23d)

I want to run away from this inner conflict...but the more I run the more I hurt.... (Nov 9th)

I can't lose you... (Feb 7th)

YES!!! YOU CAN! (Feb 7th)

I thought perhaps that you were different from the rest...joke! (Jun 6th)

My life was peaceful before you showed up!!! (Feb 19th)

I'm not sure that I made it clear to you the other night and I don't want to have any misunderstanding... (Jun 3rd)

If I'm just another woman to you then tell me...did you love me immediately? Did you know what I would be to you when you first saw me? (Dec 14th)

Hope this letter finds you well...didn't know you phoned my home a few weeks ago...the last communication from you before I shut my phone down said to, "leave me alone"...I am doing just that...wasn't being rude, didn't know you phoned...(Jul 5th)

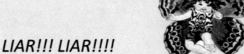

LIAR!!! LIAR!!!!
You should be inducted into the LIARS HALL OF FAME!
(Jan 22nd)

*For me to have said that I had to be out of
my mind....I have called you many
times...sorry...(Jul 5th)*

I miss you even more...
How I wished my heart was one of stone again...

How I wish that I had only one chance at love and no more...then my heart wouldn't be so disappointed...
You must have known after all these years that you would conquer my heart...and now that you have...now what?
How I wish I didn't feel like just any other woman to the man that I love with all my heart...
How can you not recognize love when it's staring you right in the face?
You said you wanted safety in a relationship...yet I don't feel safe with you...
I vowed a vow of celibacy until my husband found me and I grieve because I broke the most sacred thing to me...
I need someone that's going to be here for me...
I'm tired of other men pulling and reaching for me so hard...so tired of that until I'm crying at night ...I want to be rocked to sleep at night in your arms...
I'm tired of going to bed at night wishing you were here with me...you're someone I can unload all my secret thoughts to and not be ashamed...I'm tired of
waking up in the morning alone again...I'm tired of not being a part of someone's life...I'm tired of burning and wanting to make love...wanting to release
myself and no one's there...but you're there...your face...always...penetrating my heart to its core...I knew I'd want more...and then more...I can't... (Dec 29th)

If I'm just another woman to you then tell me...did you love me immediately? Did you know what I

would be to you when you first saw me? (Dec 14th)

**I need to say goodbye to you...I'm hurting, and I've learned that goodbye will eventually
make the pain go away... (Feb 5th)**

**Promise me you'll never forget me... (Jan 8th)
I promise...never...(Jan 8th)**

Leaving me was so damn easy for you...(Feb 28th)

*Leaving you was equivalent to an angry tsunami...everything
is destroyed now...and nothings left...(Feb 29th)*

**I AM MADDER THAN HELL WITH YOU!!! MY MOVE! BYE!
(Nov 21st)**

How could I ever have loved someone like you? (Oct 15th)

You are a dangerous woman!
(Oct 4th)

I know I'm hanging off the cliff...all by myself...

Dangerous woman! Whorish man! Thank you! Dangerous I will be! At least when I walk in the room the damned fishes don't stop swimming!
(Oct 4th)

I know what love looks like and this is not it!!! (Nov 30th)

Our fights ended like all lovers fights! You won... Again! (Sept 25th)

You hurt me...
(Dec 19th)

You should be consistent...do you want to deal with me or not? (Apr 20th)

YOU ARE MY HELL!
YOU ARE MY INSANITY!
YOU ARE MY INSANE ASYLUM!
YOU ARE MY CRAZY! Feb 28th)

I WAS FINE UNTIL YOU SHOWED UP!
YOU BROUGHT CRAZY WITH YOU!
(Nov 23rd)

I Purposely Hate You!!!
(March 9th)

Oh God, please don't leave me...
(Dec 30th)

Your visitation rights have been refused!!!! Indefinitely! (Feb 28th)

You always said I never liked you...you were right! I DON'T!
(May 4th)

I'll never forget how upset you were when you thought I was with someone else, only to be blessed with the opportunity to have me for the rest of your life...then mishandle a gift that God himself placed in your hands... (Jun 6th)

Kollye, my only crime was that I loved you... (Feb 14th)

KNOW THIS...CONTRARY TO WHAT YOU HAVE BEEN TOLD...I HAVE NEVER TRIED TO HURT OR DESTROY YOU! YOU SHOULD KNOW ME BETTER! I GUESS NOT! HOW COULD I PURPOSELY HURT SOMEONE I LOVE AS MUCH AS I LOVE YOU? FOR WHAT GAIN? BEING GULLIBLE DOES NOT BECOME YOU! (JUL 25ᵀᴴ)

LIAR!!! LIAR!!! SHAM!!!
(Oct 19ᵗʰ)

W
E
A
K
!
(Aug 6ᵗʰ)

I will not shed another tear!!! Not worth it! Not worth it! (Mar 1ˢᵗ)

IF IT WASN'T FOR GOD...I COULD HATE YOU FOREVER! EASILY! (JUL 5TH)

You are wrong! It's not your weakness that's revolting! I can deal with that! It's those bold ass lies you come up with that makes me want to vomit! (Aug3rd)

YOU ARE THE MISTAKE THAT I INTENTIONALLY MADE! NEVER HAPPEN AGAIN! (OCT 8ᵀᴴ)

I have never been so miserable as when I tried not to love you... (Oct 28ᵗʰ)

You grieve me, but I love you...
You hate every man that comes near me...but I love you...
You will never allow me to have a lover...peacefully...but I love you...
You are a promise breaker...but I love you...
You want to tear the heart out of every man that speaks to me...you jealous fool...but I love you...
You are totally possessive...and obsessive...but I love you.... (Sept 27ᵗʰ)

Sorry? You should be! I'm Not fighting over dumb sh*t no more!
(Feb 3ʳᵈ)

RAMBLINGS...

I NEED YOU...   BEHAVE!

WHAT HAVE YOU DONE TO ME?

YOU LOOK RAVISHING IN THAT RED DRESS!   I WANT YOU IN MY LIFE EVERYDAY...

BECAUSE I CARE...

I LOVE YOU IN BLACK!   THANK YOU FOR BEING SO ATTENTIVE...

YOU OWE ME DINNER...   KNOW THAT YOU ARE MY HEART...
UNPREDICTABLE AND UNTAMED YOU ARE!

I swear your mouth, lips that tongue should come with a license!

WHEN YOU WALKED INTO THAT RESTAURANT MY LEGS WENT NUMB *(Dec 1st)*

SOMEONE I CAN LOVE WITHOUT STRUGGLE... *(Oct 2nd)*
It's all lust, lust, wanton lust!   ARE YOU MY BABY?

...AND I'M FREE TO SMOTHER YOU WITH ALL OF ME...SMOTHER YOU WITH SWEET, SWEET KISSES.

THAT FACE SHOULD BE INSURED!   YOU MAKE ME FEEL SO GOOD...

I LOVE IT! YOU SMELL OF WHITE LILIES AND VIOLET LEAVES...

No matter how many others are reaching and pining for me... I only want you...
And there's no competition...

Sorry babe, I left my favorite earring in your
bedroom, please find it for me...*(Dec 23rd)*

I LONGED FOR YOU SO, TIL I THOUGHT I WOULD EXPLODE...

PROMISES, PROMISES, PROMISES...

I promise...

1. I will always love you
2. I will always keep you close to me
3. I will do everything to make you happy
4. I will take care of you
5. I will not object to you taking care of me
6. I will no longer look at handsome guys but only to declare that you are more handsome (smile)
7. I will fall asleep every night in your arms
8. I will tell you something wonderful everyday
9. I will never leave you
10. I will kiss you every day of my life
11. I will always love you

Your words caress me...your eyes sweetly kiss me...
(Sept 30th)

My heart is full of wonderful things I long to tell you...
Please don't let me overwhelm you with my own...
bottomless...stirrings... (Sept 25th)

YOU ARE GROWING MORE PRECIOUS TO ME EVERYDAY...(Aug 23rd)

Could you please fix your mouth to tell me that you love me? Please? (Sept 16th)
Babe, I love you...like crazy... (Sept 16th)

"Let me see your face, Let me hear your voice, For your voice is sweet
And your face is lovely."(Songs of Solomon 2:14b)

RAMPAGE!!!

What could have made you so angry? (May24)

I will not stop being who I am because you are uncomfortable with it! (NOV 26)

Pity...
I loved you from the beginning...pity, what a shame...you've been lying...and have lied...from the beginning... (Aug 4th)

What in the hell was I thinking when I got involved with you! What???

YOU ARE MY MADNESS!!! (Nov 15th)

What a sad day when I ceased to believe in all this love you claim you have for me! Your words are empty and sickening! You said you could never bear seeing me with another man! Forbidding me to even speak to a man! When hell freezes over! Stop your damned temper tantrums! You're old as damned dirt! Oh my God! You got rid of every man that attempted to get close to me! You conspicuously hate everyone that is near me! You cannot go blocking someone that was meant for me! How dare you! You do not own me! I am not your damned property! I have been bought and paid for by one man! Unless your first name is JESUS!!! I don't belong to you anymore my luv...YOU messed up! YOU missed your window! YOU mishandled me! So stop it! I still love you...and I always will...but I don't want you...anymore... (Jan 16th)

I've made a hard decision...I suppose I've known all along that this was not where I was supposed to be because this journey with you has been nothing but a struggle for me. You tried to pacify me last night...why come by at all? You are a Rake, pure and simple! You've caused unhappiness with your insensitive roaming nature. Unfortunately I bit the bait as others have. Unfortunately I found myself caught up in something that was never going anywhere. I found myself involved with a man that can't let go of his past relationships, all the time you keep creating new relationships and flirting incessantly because that's what Rake's do. You go from one woman to the next, from that woman to the next for what? Temporary satisfaction? You toy with people's lives and hearts! PERIOD! Don't lie and tell me that you love me ever again! What you had for me was not true love...I know what love looks like and that's not it! You got what you wanted here...now it's time to move to your next victim...the seduction here is over! It's what you've wanted after all these years...well you got it!

You are not good for me! Period!

(Mar 6th)

I will not resurrect dead relationships! (Jan 30th)

Mr. Rake! I mean it's what you do, right? I didn't love you because of who you thought you were! You reached for me and I reached back...but you DO NOT have the capacity to love me and me alone...you cannot and will not love one woman...that's not even in a Rake's vocabulary! Can't love yourself! I made the horrible mistake! Only to get here and be totally disgusted by what I have found. I'm not impressed by you! What impresses me is the caliber of a man's heart. You will never change...never unless awfully something dramatic happens...and probably not even then...you will never change it's been years and you reek of dissatisfaction to me...you should be tired of running from one woman to the next woman...I could see it in your face last night...I could smell it...you didn't have to say anything it spoke volumes...you reeked of whoredom! Aren't you tired? Don't tell me you miss ever again! Don't tell me you want me ever again! Don't tell me how long you have waited for me ever again! Yes I'm pissed off at myself for wasted time, wasted years! I'd fallen for you, those days are over boo! I promise that will never happen again, ever!!! PISSED! At myself!!!!!
(Jan 28th)

Men!!!

Some things should be sacred! Between you and me! Period! I am sick of this fighting, tired of your complaining, and damn tired of the lies, tired of the accusations! You were once my joy, my delight, my pleasure, my desire…now you are nothing but a world full of pain! (Feb 4th)

Captured

Morning,

I've discovered that love seems to be a religion all on its own...
I mean the words are often strange, incoherent and for the most part
incomprehensible to all...well...save the initiated...I asked God for
you but and I am intoxicated with your mere presence...it's the
beauty of hope and having the one thing you've wanted your whole
life in your hands...finally...you make me feel alive...I'm extremely
discriminatory when it comes to my choices...I can't just love
anybody...I was born to love only one somebody...I know that
now...thank you Lord...Thank you for showing me favor...thank
you for letting the real me surface...you're so soft and so damned
gentle I wanna holler...you're so wonderfully attentive...thank you
for desiring to please me ...Oh God...teach me how to please you...I
don't want much you've always known that...I just want to be with
you... (Sept 25th)

Call me now...need to hear your voice... (Sept 9th)

I bought you home with me...you were on my mind all night...and last night...and the night
before then...thank you for holding me...You felt soooo good...please don't make me stop next
time...I want you...incessantly...wanna feel you....I'm not afraid to love you...anymore...
you must not be afraid to let me love you...and you must not be afraid to love me...I want to
see you...Please come see me soon...Take a taxi if you have too... (Sep 30th)

You are so exquisite my dear, you are my beloved one, I love everything about you, your skin tone, your size eight
feet, that sultry voice that always sounds like your just waking from a sweet afternoon nap...your stubbornness
excites me...can't believe that I possess such an enigmatic treasure...I exalt you, my goddess...you are painfully
captivating and you have my heart... (Nov 6th)

My heart loves you... period... (Feb 3rd)

PENSIVELY PONDERING...
My biggest fear is...that I will love you too much...as I predicted I would.
My question has always been...how do I continue to restrain myself? How do
I not show how crazy I am about you? A part of me wants to go mad for you...
desire that's pent up is like a bursting dam...I wish you were my baby...many
sleepless nights I've pensively pondered in my hearts mind about you...I knew I
was falling in love with you because I wanted to make love to you incessantly,
incoherently...in the sweetest way...I need to sweetly, ravish me...I need a
rush order...I've been waiting a long time...I pray should that day ever
come that my tears don't overwhelm you... your presence alone stirs me...
you excite me...you say you go crazy whenever you see me...prove it! (Oct 1st)

You make me want to devour all of you... I love being on my knees before
you... thank God...for...pleasure... (Oct 1st)

So...no boundaries? (Sept 31st)
Babe...no boundaries... (Sept 31st)

Hey you...
You said you need my friendship...
I need yours too...(Feb 8th)

Be careful to love unbridled.....be
you....whatever that means...I can
handle whatever.......even me most
of the time...(Sept 18th)

Closeness...is why the favor was requested... (Sept 19th)
You've given me several wonderful gifts and I was always taught to never allow anyone
to be better to you than you are to them...so there are several gifts waiting for you
(smile)...talk soon....(Jun 14th)
You phoned after 3:00 a.m., I enjoy being awakened by you.... (Oct 5th)

Thank you for last night and I don't regret it...it was...sweet...every kiss, every touch, every word...they've been lingering in my hearts mind ever since...I was excited about seeing you...thank you for making my Christmas a merry one...memories of a sweet night...when I'm with you I'm so grateful to God that He made me a woman...and all the pleasures that go with it...and I love you more than you'll ever know...I will always love you ...it's been a long time for me...and I know what I need and my need and this attraction for you is stronger than I ever imagined....you are wonderful to me, you are kind towards me...if I listed the number of reasons why I love you...you've captured my heart and sometimes I don't know how to handle it, okay...I'm in a room full of people...but lonely for you... thank God for you being in my life...I couldn't have scripted it any better... every time you walk into the room my heart races...every time you phone me my heart races...when I'm in your presence I'm so overwhelmed it's because the love of my life is before me and I embrace that love with everything that I am...sometimes I'm so overwhelmed and I'm drowning in this tsunami of emotions for you...I thought at one time that I'd mastered my emotions only to encounter this avalanche of feelings that kind of blind-sided me...I just love you that's all...and most of the time love brings conflict with it...Love you always...Merry Christmas...(Dec 25th)

I will never regret loving you... (Jan 29th)

It has been the most tedious journey
With you...
But my heart only captures that part
of you that can cause it to be rendered
blind, deaf and dumb; a rumor that love proudly
adorns;
What a pity, because even then my heart
refuses to let go...why?

My heart was created to love only one...I'm in love with you and it's the kind of love that binds me so sweetly that nothing but Omnipotence could break it...I knew the day my heart loved you that I was ready then to commit for the rest of my life...and I've been patiently waiting...yes I want to make love you...I always do...and one day we will not be able to stop loving each so intensely...so passionately...so much love is so other worldly to me...it is inescapable,, it is overwhelming, it is imminent in that one day I will surrender totally...and you will too...oh God how I desperately want to...

You know I want more than just a physical relationship...I want your heart...(June 8th)

I'm not afraid anymore because you're unsure... I'm not asking for the world...I'm asking for your heart...maybe that's the world to you...? I'm willing to sacrifice everything for the one thing I've waited for ...I'm waiting to hear you say you're in love with me...I'm waiting for the day when you can step out of the fear and reach for all of me...an incredible love...an exceptional love that seemingly will not die...you will never be able to love another human being as long as you live, for you will always pine, long for me, always love me...a love that's priceless...I need you, the one I've been waiting for...I need you to reach for me as you have so many times before....don't stop reaching for me...I have always loved you...now show me... (Nov 18th)

Babe, I'm coming home as hard and fast as I can...be there soon... (Aug 24th)

Sentimental

Babe,

Six out of seven nights in the week, I sleep on the sofa···why? I hate an empty bed···when I do sleep in the bed my night is riddled with insomnia···you are supposed to be here with me···my heart loves you···I can't deny that···I long for you more than you know···to feel you···God forgive me···help me not to miss you so much.
(Oct 16th)

I recall how you
Loved me so hard for so many years··· (Oct 31st)

I PROMISE TO KEEP YOU CLOSE! (JUL 4TH)

Know what I need?

Someone I can call wonderful!

Someone I can call…mines!

(Aug 9th)

Fun watching movies with you... (Dec 6th)

Perhaps I may never be sure...
But I'm sure, that I will never be sorry...
(Jan 11th)

Just let me release this…

Awakened this morning at exactly 4:30 a.m. Wishing I had called you back…wishing you were here with me, holding me… so in case I'm awakened during the wee hours of the morning…you're there…I'm there…if nothing but to rock each other back to sleep…ever heard of…wonderful? (Nov 2nd)

I always want to hold you...

I love seeing your face...

I love your smile... (Oct 3rd)

I remember slow dancing by your fireplace...hearing you whisper that one day, you would make me your wife...and I cried...you held me so tight I could feel your whole body shaking... (Sept 21st)

The blood in my veins race at the mere sense of your presence; every emotion in me stands at attention when you look at me; every beat of

my heart answers to you...when we get really silly and laugh hysterically...love that side of you...fun times (Aug 9th)

Please tell my heart it's not wrong for loving you…
Please tell my mind to quiet down in the middle of the night…
Please tell my body that wanting you so much is not a sin…it is my right…
it is my desire…
Please keep loving me the way that you do…I'm so happy! (Dec 6th)

I don't fall in love easily…but when I do fall…I fall hard…
It took me a very long time to get to where I am with my heart…I've cried oceans of tears…
I understand that falling in love means you have to remove the chains off your heart and put it in some one else's hands…you take a chance of being hurt and having your heart ripped out by the roots…being left…you take the chance of loving someone with all your heart and that love not be reciprocated…that scares me to death…but I found out that my feelings for you and the desires of my heart far outweigh my fears…that's why when you reached for me…I reached back to you…not scared anymore to take a chance….(Aug 9th)

I could never avoid you…on purpose…when I was finally honest with myself about how I felt about you…I made a promise…that I would allow myself to love you with all that I am…no matter how foolish it may make me look…even if I fell in love …alone…I will not live with the spirit of regret for the rest of my life…so 50 years from now when I'm old and gray…I will look back and say when I had the opportunity to love you…I mean truly love you…I did… (Oct 10th) NO REGRETS

You asked me Saturday before last, "Are we going to be more than just friends?"
Yes my luv! Hell yes! (Smile) (Dec 14th)

I love the fact that I'm such a girl with you and you allow me...

I thought I'd never find you...for many years you were my dream without a face...but I claim you as the face to my prayers...I've waited patiently...not knowing if you'd even show up...or if you even existed...I'm so grateful that you're here...that you are real...I never quite believe that you are you and that I have experienced you in such a sweetly intense way...and every inch of my body that your lips hotly greeted, that your hands freely roamed to calm...and you satisfy me with an intensity that I felt rippling down my legs...make me love you so much more...I remember you asking, "Why are you breathing so hard?" Well dear it's because I thought my heart would burst...thought it would explode! For as a woman I'd given you the ultimate gift...and all I thought about was loving you...like that...forever...and you were so good to me and I wish that I could love you like that everyday...forgive me...my fear were real and not wanting to displease you was my focus...I want you to be happy too...

I want you to spoil me ...and you do. . . you know what I mean? But more than that...I want to spoil you...I want you to spend the night with me, again. . . need you...The man I dreamt about for years comes laced with a gentleness that I only found in one man...you...you have a wonderful sense of humor, love life, you love God and you have a genuine love for people...you are attentively affectionate...you are intelligent. . . you're strong and I love your handsome face. You said you didn't know where I was in all this...I love you...that is where I am...Forgive me for all my insecurities and I forgive you for yours...I'm taking the shield, the guard off my heart now because I want you to know where I am and not doubt how much I love you...know that I'm scared too but I want to trust you with my heart...okay? I want you and I want to see you...everyday...I love you and I'm reaching for you now with everything that's within me...I won't worry about tomorrow or getting hurt...I love you right now and I'm grateful to God that you are in my life...I want you in my life...

For the rest of my life... (Jan 4th)

The rain is pouring...and I can't sleep...I'm laying

here wishing things were different between us...you

want me there and I want you here...we must fix

this my luv...did my 1st movie shoot today...it was

exciting...and in the midst of all that...you were

constantly on my mind... (Feb 6th @ 8:50 a.m.)

Nostalgia

Remember the way we shared our meals?
I remember every look you have ever
given me...
I remember every touch...
I remember washing your back while you
showered then rubbing you down
with oil...I knew then that I could do
this every day for the rest of my life...be
there for you and take care of you...
I remember crying in your arms and how
you comforted me...I have always felt
safe in your arms... (September 11th -
4:08 PM)

Love spending time
you   with...at night...
at the beach...so much
fun... (April 7th)

Sitting there at the table with your friends…I was restrained I wanted to
scream and tell them just how wonderful you are...to me… (Sept 30th)

Remember when the only thing between us was forever? You promised…reminiscing, even
though you are no longer here…the woman in me still wishes I could have that
FOREVER… with you… (Jul 9th)

Babe had a blast! Luv the pub...(May 22nd)

THAT SPECIAL DAY SO LONG AGO...

I was happy and can't forget the day I first met you at many years ago...you walked up and politely asked what my name was. Do you remember that day my love? So long ago...

I reached back because you are so precious to me...you told me so many wonderful things at your house, our first date that warm September Saturday afternoon...I reached out to you because you phoned me early one morning I believe you were in Europe somewhere and you told me everything you wanted in a wife and telling me all the wonderful things a woman wants to hear...I remember how we laughed at the thought of me going topless on the beach...as we went dippy in the dome...I reached out for you because at some point you wanted to see so desperately...I reached out to you because you phoned me one night telling me 'I just love you, I just love you' but you thought I didn't love you back and I've been trying to show and convince you since then ...I reached out to you because the way you look at me...and the way you make me feel when I'm in your arms...I reached out to you because you said you loved me first, as a result causing me to love you...more... I reached out to you because I asked God for you... I don't mind taking a chance with my heart...you said I could never leave you...and I promise I won't....ever...

(Sept 25th)

I REMEMBER FEBRUARY 16…

I remember you were in Africa one Sunday morning and you called me…I love hearing your voice and knowing I could wake up to it every morning…I recall you being in London phoning me as you got on the plane telling me everything you wanted in a wife, "someone to listen to me, someone to be there for me"…and I remember so vividly every word you said and I appreciated you so much because it wasn't some outlandish expectation…it was simple, it was you…I remember the first time you held me in your arms as you were coming out of the side door of the restaurant, when you took me in your arms my knees literally buckled…

I remember hanging out at your house and how we enjoyed one another's company so…I remember how special you always made me feel…I remember at my house and showering you with love and affection… I remember your sense of humor and how hysterically funny you can be…your laughter always caused me to laugh…jokingly telling me all sorts of bizarreness…I remember you telling me that you were crazy about me, but you didn't know where I was…I remember telling you that I was in love with you that's where I was…I remember making love to you and I wanted to be there with you forever…sleepless nights come easily because I miss you …I wanted to seize every moment with you. I looked for you to tell me "I have always loved you" as many times as you wanted…you… remembered the times we've had together the many conversations…you are a joy in my life… I remember every time I ever told you that I loved you… the only thing that was missing in my life was you…and you found me…there has been no other man in my life since you…how could there be? You love me so intensely that I have no recollection of ever loving anyone else…All I remember now is you…

I remember the time you just called…to say "hi…I care about you"…. you have always been so unusually kind to me…..I remember every kiss, every stare, every smile, every hug, every meal shared, every fireplace conversation (love those)…I remember every fight, every tear, every "I'm sorry"…

I remember the times when your joy seems to bubble over and I want to see that again… I was scared to love you so much and you told me and showed how afraid you were to love me…we were both afraid of getting hurt…I've never felt so much pain…I'm hurting now…but I believe there's a piece of heaven on earth and I want you in my life…never ever thought I would be jealous…I remember you loving me at your house the last time I was there…every night since I have remembered THAT night…no one holds a candle to you…I remember and you've always told me that you are the best at what you do…and I concur…every plea for me to come back to you…I remember everything…most of all I remember the first love letter you wrote me on that warm, sunny day in September…

I remember and I shall never forget… (February 2nd[th])

Missing you terribly…we have shared some of the gladdest days together…(Mar 30th)

Tell me how not to need you so much…it's killing me
sweetly… (Feb 24th)

Memories…sometimes they are much too painful for me to

remember…(Feb 20th)

Longings...

*Forgive me if I conspicuously
expressed how much I wanted to be
in your arms yesterday
morning...it's a place I've been
longing to be in since the last time
I saw you...just a few hours ago
(smile)... I just want you here
with me...sorry I had to pull
away because I knew I'd want to
stay and never let you go...*
(Nov 30th)

*Sitting in your office waiting for you, and my heart is racing...
We have loved each other for years and I still get excited every time I see you...
every time the phone rings and you are on the other end,
every time you walk through the door...
it feels as if these strong desires for you will be with me...forever...
keep waiting for them to quieten down, subside...I'm still waiting...
they soothe my mind...you're more to me than just a play thing...there's more to me than
the longings of my fleshly desires...I'm waiting for this rage to calm down...in the meanwhile,
I won't run for I cannot run from myself...dying to be touched by you... You mesmerize me...I
Believe it's because...you are my fantasy...I have a face now...I dream of a sweet surrender
that's like a long awaited summer storm...one day...I pray...*
Summer storm
(March 13)

Somewhere out across the Atlantic my baby is missing…have you seen him? He's this tall debonair…handsome fellow that left the west coast and took my heart with him…he phone once…but we got disconnected…if you see him…tell him…that I can't live without my heart…nor do I want to live without him…(Nov 19th)

There is only one person on planet earth that I long for… (Oct 22nd)

How ironic for you to phone and ask,
"What are we going to be?"
Just this morning I had an extra key made for my apartment…
to give to you…
and I thought to myself if I give him this key…then he's definitely
more than a friend to me…
I'm crazy about you too…what are we going to be?
Must you ask again?
(Dec 6th)

Love is a language all its own…I melt every time you call me "BABY"… (May 9th)

Shall I go mad with this incessant longing for you? God make it stop! (Dec 15th)

Facsimiles...

ENAMORED – page 9

You can't love me the way you did on Saturday and not expect me to want more...I'm saved...not dead...especially around you...I'm still a sexual woman...I can feel...I know where I am...you excite me...it's not manipulation...you always told me I had the liberty to be me and to say what I wanted to you...if you want me to tone it down...it's like sitting on a simmering volcano and an explosive eruption is imminent....you validate my feelings because you've allowed me to express them to you...I promise you I'm not trying to displease God with my behavior...and this is not a poor attempt to seduce a beautiful man...it's against God's laws to have sex outside of marriage...I understand all the repercussions and consequences that follow fornication...been there done that....and I also know that by loving you I risk the chance of getting my heart broken again...but I also have the chance to have one of the greatest experiences of my life...I am in a place that I haven't been in, in years....I'm in love....and I'm reaching for the man in you....and I strongly desire you ...I was made to be loved...it's not easy being in your presence and I can't touch you and then fight with everything that's within me to control my urges for you....they are real and I cannot deny they are here...I live with them every day....when I don't see you they are there...in the night they are there....in the daytime they are there....and they are involuntary...so I turn to you....I'm relieved when I express myself to you.... I want you....not your stuff...YOU...I knew I loved you I just wasn't sure how much until the longings increased and I found myself on my knees begging God to relieve me of this....newfound torment....they say you obsess over me...it becomes you (smile)...I do know that you are very possessive...I don't mind at all, in fact I welcome it with open arms... (Sept 16th)

AMORED – page 9

Just sitting here in the wee hours of the morning listening to Luther Vandross reflecting back over this past year...I'm thankful for my life...it may not be all that I'd hoped for right now and perhaps many dreams have not yet been realized but I'm grateful for my life...I've held on and I'm still here....I feel more alive...there are no other arms I'd rather be in...the last time you were at my apartment, licking m nose...I knew then as I know now that for too long I have denied myself of I remember you smothering me with kisses the one thing that I needed most as a woman...I long to be spoiled by you...you know what I mean? Spoil me with you... I can't go another day like that...I'm not weak...I'm a woman...you are so strong in my heart...I feel empty when you're not around...ever felt "emptiness" before? I appreciate you...didn't know I wouldn't be able to let go of you...and I don't want to...ever....riding on the train I thought about you...saw two people kissing and I thought about you...walked in my room and I thought about you...listening to Dee Harvey sing and I thought about you...walked by a fish tank and thought about you...saw an airplane take off and I thought about you...always on my hearts mind... (Dec 1st)

SMITTEN – page 11

Hollye, Hollye, Oh Hollye!

(Dec 23rd)

CONFLICT – page 28

It's almost 4am...can't sleep...I was anxious to see you, why didn't you call to say were not coming? You are dear to my heart, know that I would rather die a thousand deaths than to hurt you, regardless to what your friends and the enemy has said...I care about you...and I want you in my life...All I have to offer is my love...for the rest of your life, love you and take care of you like the king that you are... (Mar 7th)

Facsimiles cont'd . . .

INSATIABLE – page 18

It's not easy being in your presence and I can't touch you or you won't look at me...or fight with everything that's within me to control my urges for you....they are real and I cannot deny they are here...I live with them every day....when I rarely see you they are there...in the night they are there....in the daytime they are there....and they are involuntary...so I turn to you....I am relieved when I express myself to you.... I want you....YOU...I knew I loved you I just wasn't sure how much until the longings increased and I found myself on the floor begging God to relieve me of this....new found torment....so I bury myself in my work and other things...but you are the biggest distraction I have...God help me... (Sept 16th)

LONGINGS – page 46

I was alone for a very long time...for many years...thirteen to be exact, when you came into my life...so my response to you is not out of desperation...sitting here in the wee hours of the morning listening to Luther Vandross reflecting back over this past year...I'm thankful for my life....I feel more alive than ever...there are no other arms I'd rather be in but yours...the last time you were at my apartment, licking my nose...I knew then as I know now for far too long, what I have denied myself of. I remember you smothering me with kisses the one thing that I needed most...I long to be spoiled by you...you know what I mean? Spoil me with you... I can't go another day like that...I'm not weak...I'm human...you are so strong in my heart...I feel empty when you're not around...ever felt "emptiness" before? I appreciate you...didn't know I wouldn't be able to let go of you...and I don't want to...ever....riding on the train I thought about you...saw two people kissing I thought about you...walked in my room looking at that queen size bed...and I thought about you...listening to Dee Harvey sing and I thought about you...walked by a fish tank and thought about you...saw an airplane take off and I thought about you...always on my mind...can't stop thinking about you...(Dec 1st)

CONLFLICT – page 28

Why am I here in your life? Why was I ever here? Am I like everybody else? Surely to me you are unlike any person on planet earth that I've ever known. Did I walk through the wrong door? Have I misinterpreted God's voice? What have I done to my heart? Did I surrender to the wrong heart? Is my heart hurting now because this was never meant to be in the first place? Was I wrong in reaching back to you because you reached for me first? What am I to you? How do I find my way back? Back to where I was before you...You're all my heart knows...why in the hell do I miss you? I question every second my heart ever loved you...don't even attempt to define your love for me...dammit you already have! I'm done!!! (July 9th)

SENTIMENTAL – page 40

Hello Gorgeous,

First of all, I want to thank you for being so kind to me and I want you to know that all those feelings are mutual. I've been thinking about you a lot often and wondered how you and your son were doing. I must admit I was a little hurt after I found out you were married and had a little girl, but trying to get your divorce. But don't worry, I'll be alright o.k. I just hope you're alright. You have to hang in there and just hope things will get better. I really miss you and I'll always love you. I'm going through some tough times right now because my job is commission only. I don't eat unless I make a sell. But I'm going to hang in there. I will just keep writing and don't get yourself into trouble. I do now and always will love you. I still love you. Me (Feb 13th)

RAMPAGE – page 35

I wanted a man that understands love, love changes people for the better…it adds to their lives, it brings blessings and a wealth of riches that money could never buy. I want a man in my life that has the capacity to love and COMMIT to me and me alone, and no that's not a four-letter word, perhaps to you it might be but I never thought I'd see the time when you would come to me and I didn't want you or want to touch you and love you…because I'd missed you so much…but to my surprise…last night…I could see other women in your face…hear them in your mind, they are all over you…you are infested with other women…and you need help…I'm going to pray for you…I'm sorry I can't give my heart to a man that simply is not worthy of it…I wanted you not a game, I wanted a life with you and no one else, but you make other men look like giants…and make yourself look so small, why ? Why? Not you too…

I loved you with every fiber of my being only to have you mock my love…I let go of so many fears just for you…I loved you so much but you neither give nor have you learned how to receive my love…money and sex doesn't equal love…I can have sex with anybody, just pick up the phone…or have it by myself! But I love you and not wanting you when that's all I dream about is hurting me…last night I had no desire for you…I mean I prayed for us to spend time together…all I wanted was to show you that you are the only man I've wanted and getting here has broken me down. I've cried many tears because I was afraid but I loved you anyway…many times I've crawled to you but I followed my heart with you…dumb ass heart…many nights I've suffered because I was so lonely for you…I opened up to you…where is my baby? Where is the man I love? Where is the man I couldn't keep my hands off of? Where is the man that went to hell and back just to get me? Where is the man that I prayed for? Where are you? Where is my baby? I'm just scared that I will never find him… I am looking for my king…is there a man that can love one woman above the rest? Is there? Is there a man that can commit to one woman only? Is there a man that knows how to be satisfied with one woman for the rest of his life? Is there a man that doesn't think marriage is a prison sentence? Is there a man that can love me and only me? YES, there is…and next time I will never let him go, whoever the hell he is! (Jan 30th)

RAMPAGE – page 35

What do you do when your Judas is still alive?

My life has always been a very private one…I thought I was going to die and actually wanted to when I was betrayed…why? It was equivalent to dropping the Little Boy Bomb on my soul. How do you fight a betrayer? Pray for them…I have never been more embarrassed, humiliated, mortified, ashamed and so lonely that I could not articulate…and the depth of my loneliness is beyond words…No way I could remain placid or pretend as if my life was undisturbed by such betrayal…and to have my pain mocked by your friends who don't know me and never knew me…but YOU know me…or at least I thought you did…my life will never be the same again…the trauma of this whole incident has changed me…I've cried tears I didn't know I had…many days I couldn't get out of bed…and I prayed for God to help me…and now your voice sounds like gibberish to me…just blowing hot air…saying nothing! Blah, blah, blah, blah, blah! Of no consolation…at all! To hell with your "I'M SORRY!" You don't understand… do you think someone I've waited my whole life for…do you really believe I would get here…finally…then destroy the very thing I've waiting for? I've dreamed about you… and thought the world was dead without you….it's like that…or was like that….Surely the devil didn't order an assignment for me to love you or for you to love me…can there be love and God not be in it? I don't think so…Have our souls met? I really don't think so… (Nov 30th)

CONFLICT – page 28

When I received that letter from you...I literally got up from my desk, walked outside don't know how because I remember my thighs growing numb...thought I was trippin'...went back to the letter only to find those words were real...so I said all that to say...all of this didn't start off "calm" for me...you planted those words into my spirit...little did you know that I would respond the way that I have and now that I have...you apparently don't know what to do with me or it's all a part of the game...you can't go around toying with people's hearts...then laugh about it at some round table discussion...or get pissed off if you think I'm seeing someone else...I'm boggled by you...

I realize that we are not in the same place...you are not ready for me, for whatever reason, it really doesn't matter. We operate in a totally different dimension...I know where my heart is, and I know what love looks like... you said you don't know where your heart is and you haven't taken out the time to monitor it...you said you don't even think about happiness...the question has to be, why? After all this time I still feel empty...I'm not sure if that's a reflection of spending time with you, if so how do you live like that? Pouring my heart out to you I didn't realize until now that it has always felt like I was pouring feelings into a colander...only to be told indirectly that it's not okay to be me and say what's on my heart to you...I think you'd rather I take your money or gifts then ask for your heart...

Loving many men at one time was never my forte...being whorish is not me. I will never apologize for not being like other women...I knew long ago that you were incapable of loving with all your heart...but that's what I need...a whole man or one that's at least reaching for wholeness...broken men hurt women...men with deep issues destroy women's lives...men that run from woman to woman are weak...it speaks volumes, one, that you don't know what you really want so you take anything and everything that's available...yes a real man handles responsibilities and a real man also has a heart and the capacity to give as well as take...a real man can love one woman and be completely satisfied...you try to come off as a roaring lion...when in fact you're everything but!

We started off intense as far as I'm concerned...I know how to have fun with you, at the beach, shooting pool, playing basketball, doing a movie, dancing on top of the hood of a car, playing strip poker, going to plays, operas, baseball games, karaoke, picnics at the park or on my living room floor, playing dress up, comedy shows you name it...hey we started off with the "I love you's"...only thing I asked you was if you wanted me to love you, because many times men won't open their mouths and let women know they don't want them...nothing is said but you show it in your actions... and most of the time women spend years hoping, wishing and dreaming for something that's long been dead...I thought I could trust you...I thought you were cool as hell...I thought you were different from the rest... ...I fell for you because you told me that you have always loved me...that was all I needed...so forgive me for not being "calm" and "relaxed"...forgive me for being excited even if it lasted only a short while...I thought you were the man that would be in my life...chalk it up to naïveté... I understand...if you really wanted me in your life I would be with you... (Jun 24th)

CONFLICT – page 28

*I know what love looks like...you keep changing and I keep adjusting...you're not the same man that you were in the beginning and that makes me sad....but I adjusted... you talk a good game and the package is beautiful on the outside, but when I reached for you on the inside I was shocked at what I found...and I've adjusted...I'm here because of what you said...no other reason...remember what **you** said...I only responded...to what you declared to me... (January 29th)*

ACKNOWLEDGEMENTS

TEXTUAL

Every effort has been made to locate all copyright holders. In the event that we have unwillingly or inadvertently omitted the proper notification, the author would be grateful to hear from the copyright holder and to amend the following editions accordingly.

The author gratefully acknowledges the permission of the following to reproduce copyrighted material in this book: Cover Image - Angel Blue Sad Mourning – Angel Lost Love by Kathy Fornal-Fine Art America © 2014; Seasons Linens Poem– Author/Poemist Antwan Hannah - © 2014;

ILLUSTRATIVE

Inside Cover Artwork created by: Luthien Thye-"My Heart Will Go On" - Mixed Media Journal-Malaysia-© 2014; Pictures on intro page and pages 2, 3, 7, 11, 12, 18, 19, 25, 26, 31, 32, 43, 44, 46, 47, 49, 54, 55, Vintagefeedsack.blogspot.com-(Prior to 1923) ℗ Pictures on pages 5, 22, 28, 36, 37, 38, GraphicsFairy.com℗; Pictures on pages 5, 13, 14, 16, 24, 27, 29, 31, 34, Karenwhimsy.com℗; Pictures on pages 4, 14, Vintageholidaycrafts.com Picture on page 2, created by Hollye Lexington (Author);

Page 6 artwork courtesy of the late Alfonse Maria Mucha (1860-1939), "Winter" 1897; Seasons series "Spring & Summer" 1898; Stone Series, "Topaz" 1900 ℗ Wikipaintings.org; Page 8 artwork courtesy of the late Evelyn De Morgan (1855-1919), "Demeter Mourning for Persephone" 1906 ℗Wikipaintings.org; Page 10 artwork courtesy of the late Lord Frederick Leighton (1830-1896), "Acme & Septimius"1868 ℗Wikipaintings.org; Page 11 artwork courtesy of the late William Adolphe Bougeriau (1825-1905), "The Abduction of Psyche" 1889℗Wikipaintings.org; Page 20 artwork courtesy of the late Lord Frederick Leighton (1830-1896), "Wedded" (1881-1882) Commons.Wikimedia.org; ℗ Page 23 artwork courtesy of the late Lord Frederick Leighton (1830-1896), "Fishermen & the Syren" (1856-1858)℗Commons.Wikimedia.org; Page 27 artwork courtesy of the late Lord Frederick Leighton (1830-1896), "Clytie" (1885 1886), ℗ Wikipaintings.org; Page 30 courtesy of the late Sir Edward Burne-Jones (1833-1898), "Love Among the Ruins", (1873)℗ Commons.Wikimedia.org; Picture on page 33 courtesy of Sir Edward Burne-Jones (1833-1898), "Temperantia" (1872),℗ WikimediaCommons.org; Picture on page 34 courtesy of the late Sir Lawrence Alma-Tadema (1836-1912), "Her eyes are with her thoughts and they are far away", (1897) ℗Wikipaintings.org; Picture on page 38 courtesy of the late Sir Lawrence Alma-Tadema (1836-1912), "A Balneator" (1877)℗ The Anthenaeum.org; Page 39 courtesy of the late Evelyn De Morgan (1855-1919), "Luna", (1885)℗ Commons.Wikimedia.org; Picture on page 40 courtesy of Hermitage Museum, courtesy of artist Il Somoma (1477-1549) "Cupid" 1500's℗; Picture on page 41 courtesy of the late Alfonse Maria Mucha (1860-1939), "Flowers" (1897)℗Commons.Wikimedia.org; Picture on page 42 courtesy of Sir Frederick Leighton (1830-1896), "Flaming June", (1895)℗ Wikipaintings.org; Picture on page 44 courtesy of the late Alfonse Maria Mucha (1860-1939), "Evening Reverie" (1898) ℗ Wikipaintings.org; Picture on page 48 courtesy of the late Evelyn De Morgan (1855-1919), "In Memoriam", (1898)℗ (Source Common.Wikimedia.org; Author Photographed by Ta-Nae Sanders of Chii-Q Photography.

Epilogue

LONGINGS – *page 46*

I dream of sleeping underneath you every saying my name...how I love waking up me... thankful that I have your heart ...the you will ever know...you love me in a way really care for me...I love that...your love is close but sometimes yet so far away...I ever told me...I can't forget that...and I ask hook me probably for life? The caused me many sleepless nights and so words alive in my hearts mind? How do I have responded to you in the only way I that has astonished even me...Why am I in Surely I couldn't be more open...and I feel not some figment of my imagination...no arms, loved you with my body, missed you

night...to hear your heart beat, hear your voice every morning and seeing you lying next to way you have mines...it is a blessing more than that blows my mind...you show how much you so intense and I love it! Having my blessing so cannot forget all the wonderful things you you, didn't you know that those words would psychological effects of those words have much happiness...how do I function with those compartmentalize that? How do I respond? I know how...I have opened my heart in a way your life? Why am I having this experience? extremely vulnerable and exposed...you are you are real to me...I have held you in my like crazy when you're gone...miss the hell out

of you... I've experienced you and I love you more than I did when this all first began...why did our paths cross? I prayed for the man of my dreams and you are that man...I didn't know it at first now I know...still miss you...wishing you were here with me...Thank you babe for every love letter...you will forever be near and dear to my heart... (Sept 18th)

> *I will not rebel against my heart, it is my soul...and I cannot rise against my mind for it is my divine sense...*
> *(Dec 14th)*
>
> ~Ta-Nae Sanders

Love is a religion all its own...

Hollye Lexington's gift book, "Secret, Sacred Love Letters" is the first of its kind from the author. An enchanting, irresistible compilation of personal love letters that span over four decades, from 1973 - 2013. Years in the making this delightful, amorous journey will usher you into a world of love, volcanic emotions, conflict, desire, and heart wrenching heartbreak, intensity and unconditional passion. The content provides an alluring combination of beauty, nostalgia and romance. Secret, Sacred Love Letters is graciously inspired by the love experience and trustingly speaks to true lovers everywhere.

To create the book, beautiful illustrations were researched for months and you will be pleasured by gifted artists that cover the globe. Letters from the early 1970's are poured into this alluring mixture of quotations and love letters that will fuel the fire of lovers everywhere and promises to tug at every emotion and heartstring for anyone who has ever passionately loved with all their heart.

Inspired by Michelle Lovric's book 'Passionate Love Letters, Anthology of Desire' written in 1996. Hollye Lexington is also the author of an e-book entitled: "From Heartbreak to Worship". Secret, Sacred Love Letters has been a pet project for many years and its completion has been a dream come true. The author is in great anticipation of her next book which is near and dear, entitled: "Whole Woman Now."
Hollye Lexington is the mother of two adult children and resides in Long Beach, California.

Cover Image: Angel Blue Sad Mourning – Angel Lost Love by Kathy Fornal- Fine Art America © 2014

Inside Cover Artwork created by: Winnie Luthien Thye-Mixed Media Journal-Malaysia © 2014

Author Photographed by Ta-Nae Sanders of Chii-Q Photography

Published by AuthorHouse

Secret Sacred Love Letters

This book is dedicated to the one true love of my life...

Printed in the United States
By Bookmasters